The Ripple Effect

How You Can Make A Difference To The World Every Day

TONY RYAN

A HeadFirst Publication

1st print: August 1999
2nd Print: February 2000
3rd Print: December 2000
4th Print: June 2001
5th Print: April 2004

© Tony Ryan 1999

This Book Is Copyright

Apart from any fair dealing for the purposes of research, private study, criticism or review, as permitted under the Copyright Act, no part may be reproduced by any process without written permission from the publishers.

Exemption is granted for the purchaser of this book to make individual photocopies of the quotes on the left side pages for display purposes.

National Library of Australia
Cataloguing-in-Publication data:

Ryan, Tony.

The Ripple Effect: How you can make a difference to the world every day.

Bibliography.
ISBN 0 9577267 0 8

1. Example. 2. Helping behaviour. 3. Influence.
(Psychology). 4. Change. 5. Causation.   I. Title.

116

The printing of this book was proudly undertaken by McPherson's Printing Group.

The magic cover was superbly designed by Tanya Euler of Orator Corporation.

Each of us can make a positive difference to the world with what we do every day. Nowhere is this more evident than with my wife Sharon, who changes so many lives for the better with her daily actions. So, to this beautiful woman, I dedicate this book.

Some acknowledgments to people who have created ripples in my own life

The following people made a significant difference to the writing of this book. It probably would not have taken shape without their support and advice.

To Alie Blackwell, for encouraging me over the years to sit down and produce this book. I'd still just be talking about it if it wasn't for you.

To Diane Furness, thank you for your wonderful editing advice. You have a gift with words and ideas.

To my sister, Tricia O'Neill, and to great friend, Tony Banks, for offering to read the earlier drafts and then giving your superb feedback.

To Cheryll Beaumont, the best typesetter in the world, who braved the countless rewritings and continually offered great suggestions for improvements.

And especially to my lover (and wife) Sharon, who lived with me through the full writing process, and still loves me in spite of it.

My heartfelt thanks to every one of you for choosing to make a difference with what you did.

How You Can Make A Difference To The World Every Day

Words into actions

50 per cent of all profits from the sale of *The Ripple Effect* will be donated to registered community charities that offer direct assistance to disadvantaged children in Australia. Thus, even your purchase of this book will make a small difference to the world.

For details on applying for these funds, please refer to this book's web-site on:

www.headfirst.com.au/ripples/

CONTENTS

PREFACE 1

**UNDERSTANDING THE RIPPLES:
How and why the ripple effect works** 5

    Can one person *really* make a difference? 7

    Why it is so important for you
    to believe in the ripple effect 11

    Personal perspectives on the ripple effect 13

    Global perspectives on the ripple effect 27

    Key points about the ripple effect 43

**SPREADING THE RIPPLES:
Ideas for making a difference
to the world every day** 47

    1. Take personal responsibility 51

    2. Do volunteer work 55

    3. Purchase wisely 61

    4. Watch what you say 65

    5. Make every action count 69

    6. Really listen to others 75

7. Believe in your own talents 79
8. Reflect on your actions 83
9. Look for the good in others 87
10. Create new ideas 93
11. Look after yourself 97
12. Write encouraging messages 101
13. Find your natural pace 107
14. Focus on your own family 113
15. Re-discover your spirit 117
16. Enjoy the work of your life 121
17. Spread unconditional love 127
18. Connect @ the Net 131
19. Live in the present moment 137
20. Bring people together 145

Some pebbles to toss in the pond:
Things you can do right now 153

Appendix I: Origin of the ripple concept 182
Appendix II: About the author 183

The Ripple Effect

> *Every day you are tested a hundred times: are you going to help this planet or hurt it? People wince when you say that, but it should be a comforting thought. It means everything you do matters.*
> (Brian Hall)

PREFACE

You can make a difference with your everyday actions. Listen to the stories told around our planet, and you will hear this message over and over again.

All of those little things you do in every moment of your life can ripple out to create endless changes in the lives of others, and there is no need to become a politician, or a famous author, to have such a powerful effect. One of your tiny actions this very day could ripple out and make a positive change to the world.

And does the world need changing? Yes it does. While there are many wonderful aspects to being alive today, there are also many overwhelming dilemmas, be they social, environmental or spiritual. They need to be addressed by each of us if we hope to create a more sustainable future for our children.

In your own small way, you can choose to take part of the responsibility for creating some of the changes that can resolve these dilemmas. The price you pay for living on this planet is to contribute to its welfare with the skills you have.

Unfortunately, in the modern era, it is sometimes difficult to believe that you have the power to create those changes.

The Ripple Effect

> Each time a man stands up for an idea,
> or acts to improve the lot of others,
> or strikes out against injustice, he sends
> forth a tiny ripple of hope, and crossing
> each other from a million different
> centers of energy and daring, those
> ripples build a current that can
> sweep down the mightiest walls
> of oppression and resistance.
>
> (Robert F. Kennedy)

Several hundred years ago, you may have lived in a small village of a few hundred people. Your world would have extended no further than the visible horizon, and your individual efforts would have created a noticeable effect within such a tiny group.

But today, your world *is* the entire world. In a global community of six billion people, there just seems to be too much to deal with out there. In this twenty-first century environment, it is much more difficult to believe that you have the personal power to create significant change.

And yet, all human endeavours throughout history have been attained by individuals who knew that they could make a difference. Their efforts were based upon their hope that they could create a better world up ahead. If we collectively lose that hope, then we will indeed struggle to resolve those dilemmas facing us in the world today.

To rediscover that hope, you must believe in your personal power to create ripples that spread out and change the world. In fact, if it is not you who is going to do it, then who else do you think is likely to make the effort? Remember that every change on this planet begins with a human being somewhere, somehow. It may as well be you.

*The small things in everyday life
are no less sacred than the
great issues of human existence.*
(Thomas Moore)

UNDERSTANDING THE RIPPLES:

How and why the ripple effect works

> *What is a ripple? It is the inside-out release of energy generated by your thoughts and actions that eventually affects the lives of other people in some way. This energy connects with the ripples from the thoughts and actions of others to create all of the daily events on this planet.*

If you think you are too small to be effective, you have never been in bed with a mosquito.

(Bette Reese)

Can one person *really* make a difference to the world?

Absolutely. Because of the exponential effect of the ripples, one of your seemingly insignificant actions can indeed change the lives of many other people. Wars have begun with little more than a harsh word being directed at another person.

At the same time, there are other instances in which, to create change, your tiny contribution must converge with many others. It is rarely possible for you to individually affect a major long-term crisis, such as the war on drugs in your country, or environmental pollution in your own city.

Though you may not individually bring about direct major change with issues of this magnitude, there are still many ways of steadily making a positive contribution. For instance, consider these two approaches to the issue of air pollution:

The DIRECT Approach. Instead of driving your car as a sole occupant, take a bus to work each day. Remind yourself that a bus full of passengers replaces the need for 48 cars to be on the freeway. This means that every month and a half, you have saved the equivalent of 48 cars being on the road.

You have eliminated the pollution created by the removal of a single car each day from the city's freeways. This may not seem very much, but if you theoretically compressed those 48 days into one day, you would be preventing a line-up of 48 cars over three hundred metres long on that day. Consider this in terms of traffic congestion, and also of the air pollution that is created.

Each small part of everyday

life is part of the total

harmony of the universe.

(St. Theresa of Lisieux)

The INDIRECT Approach. Engage in positive conversations with other people when you are talking about personal efforts in preventing air pollution. You may influence them to think likewise, and eventually hundreds of others may do something about the issue.

My wife Sharon is superb at this. In conversations with others, she will plant positive seeds of encouragement at every opportunity. I regularly listen in awe as she creates an atmosphere of support for an issue, simply with some quiet words. As people leave, I can see them nodding in support, and ready to enlist others in the cause. Who knows how far those words of hers may eventually spread?

The Ripple Effect

I am done with great things and big plans, great institutions and big success. I am for those tiny, invisible loving human forces that work from individual to individual, creeping through the crannies of the world like so many rootlets, or like the capillary oozing of water, yet which, if given time, will rend the hardest monuments of human pride.

(William James)

Why it is so important for you to believe in the ripple effect

- It gives you *hope* for the future. When you know that you can create change for yourself and others, you overcome the sense of helplessness imposed by a complex world.

- You will feel better about yourself, and derive more *satisfaction* from your everyday existence, when you believe that you can make a positive difference to life on the planet.

- It encourages you to take *responsibility* for your actions, rather than blaming others for your troubles.

- When you realise that you can create changes with your efforts, it can give you the *confidence* to go outside your comfort zone and attempt new activities.

- At the end of your life, you will know that you have left a *legacy* for future generations.

- You can realise that you don't have to become rich, famous or behave in extreme ways to change the world. You can do so with your small seemingly *insignificant* actions every day.

How lovely to think that no one need wait a moment: we can start now, start slowly changing the world! How lovely that everyone, great and small, can make a contribution towards introducing justice straightaway.

(Anne Frank)

Personal perspectives on the ripple effect

How do the ripples work in our daily reality? Consider this example. A female friend of mine once noticed a distraught young mother nursing a crying baby at a shopping centre cafeteria. My friend bought a cup of tea, presented it to the mother, and offered to nurse her baby for a few minutes.

A little later, both mother and baby had calmed down. The young woman thanked my friend for her efforts, and they parted.

Several weeks later, a letter appeared in the local newspaper. It was written by the woman who had been so distraught at the shopping centre cafeteria.

In this letter, she explained that she had been crying because she had planned to suicide, and did not know what to do with her baby.

However, my friend's single action had been enough to boost her into positive action and, since the time in the cafeteria, she had managed to create new purposes in her life. Both mother and baby, she explained, were doing well.

What is the use of living if it not be to strive for noble causes and to make this muddled world a better place for those who will live in it after we are gone?
(Winston Churchill)

Imagine all of the occasions, every day, that you set off ripples in this manner. They will be the specific moments when you make choices that create changes in the world around you.

There may be hundreds of these instances in your life every day. In most cases, it is when you are making connections with another human being. When my friend approached the young mother and offered her the cup of tea, this was a critical turning point.

In the following pages are some possible scenarios from everyday life. As you read them, remember that they are only a tiny slice of the potential consequences that could have resulted from the turning points.

The Ripple Effect

You can't live a perfect day without doing something for someone who will never be able to repay you.
(John Woden)

7.00 a.m. — Breakfast

The scenario:
Everyone is rushing about, attempting to prepare themselves for the day. The children, as usual, are struggling to climb out of bed.

The turning point:
In spite of your frustration with your children for being late, you directly compliment your youngest child at the breakfast table. "Thank you," you say, "for your great effort with your homework last night."

The ripple effect:

—> The child goes quiet, and flushes slightly at the praise

—> she goes to school, and enters her classroom feeling happy with herself and her world

—> her teacher notices the increased confidence, and asks her to try a difficult maths problem

—> your child completes it, and her teacher feels elated at the success

—> the teacher is encouraged to persist with looking for the good things that her students can achieve

—> the children have an inspiring day

—> they all go home in an uplifted mood and spread their positive energy within their families, including yours.

The Ripple Effect

Give me a lever long enough...

and single-handed I can

move the world.

(Archimedes)

8.10 a.m. — Driving along the freeway

The scenario:
As you enter the freeway, you discover that the traffic is heavier than usual, and is moving quite slowly. You then notice that the young driver in the car beside you is trying to enter your lane, because her exit is coming up. No-one is letting her in, and she is becoming tense and upset.

The turning point:
You stop, and wave her through in front of you with a flourish and a smile.

The ripple effect:

—> She returns your smile, acknowledges your thoughtful action, and drives on

—> her tension dissipates, and she arrives at her company office feeling buoyed by your little effort

—> as the main receptionist, she is the first to greet the hundreds of people who enter the office each day

—> with her positive greeting, she decides to brighten up the life of every person she meets throughout that day

—> because of her efforts, many others in the business district are inspired to focus on their own positive efforts.

Do not be afraid to take a big step if one is required. You can't cross a chasm in two small steps.

(Chinese saying)

8.40 a.m. — Arrival at work

The scenario:
Many of your fellow workers have congregated in the staff room, drinking tea or coffee, and are complaining about the excesses of their present programs.

The turning point:
You briefly refer to the merits of one of these programs, and acknowledge one man in particular who has contributed an excellent component of that program.

The ripple effect:

—> He is boosted by your comments, and returns to his desk to begin his day's work

—> soon after, his phone rings, and an angry caller demands an apology for the poor service he received from the company the previous day; this poor service had adversely affected the caller's own business causing him to lose sales

—> however, because of the positive mood generated by your earlier comment in the staff room, the man placates the caller, and promises to arrange a free personalised service that same morning

—> as a result of his efforts, the caller decides not to take legal action that he is entitled to against the company, an action that would have cost them over $50 000 in an out-of-court settlement.

It is the greatest of all mistakes to do nothing because you can only do a little. Do what you can.

(Sydney Smith)

1.15 p.m. — Lunch break

The scenario:
You have lined up at a nearby snack bar, a shop well-known for its excellent food. Because such an effort is made with the food preparation, it is necessary to wait for more than ten minutes. Others in the line are complaining openly about the delays.

The turning point:
As you purchase your sandwiches, you smile at the shop manager and thank her for creating such excellent food, making certain that the other customers can hear you.

The ripple effect:

—> The shop manager has been feeling overwhelmed by the negative comments, yet is re-energised by your positive words

—> she chats and jokes with the next customer, who happens to be embroiled in an ongoing dispute in her own office

—> when this customer returns to her office, she feels impelled to finally sort out the dispute; calling everyone together, she initiates a more positive approach to the arguments and, within days, the dispute has been resolved.

The Ripple Effect

> *The only thing needed for evil to triumph is for good men to do nothing.*
>
> *(Oliver Wendell Holmes)*

7.50 p.m. — Attending a local community meeting

The scenario:
There has recently been an increased number of burglaries in your neighbourhood, and one of your neighbours has arranged a meeting to lobby for an increased police presence in your area. Although you are tired from your day's work, you attend the meeting.

The turning point:
You give a brief speech offering your support for your neighbour's proposal.

The ripple effect:

—> Your support convinces others in attendance to sign a protest letter

—> the letter is delivered to the inspector in charge of police in your region

—> several months later, more police are allocated to patrol in your neighbourhood

—> days later, the presence of one of these officers late at night discourages a burglar from breaking into your own home.

The creation of a thousand forests is in one acorn.

(Ralph Waldo Emerson)

Global perspectives on the ripple effect

Three special global understandings form a basis for the ripple effect. They are:

1. Ripples expand exponentially

One tiny action can spread out to create massive changes.

2. Everything is connected

All life forms on planet Earth are connected through a common spiritual web of existence.

3. What goes around comes around

The consequences of your actions can later return and affect you in some way.

A mighty flame

followeth a tiny spark.

(Dante)

1. The exponential power of the ripples

In the twenty-third century, an eminent scientist invented the first time machine in the Earth's history. He excitedly clambered into this new device, and travelled back over five hundred years until he found himself in the middle of a beautiful forest.

Climbing out of the machine, he began to walk along a path, when he suddenly noticed a strange and beautiful flower growing nearby. Reaching down, he plucked this flower, and only then saw the sign that said: "Please. Do not pick the flowers."

Overcome with regret, he ran back to his machine, and set the controls that would return him to his own time. When he arrived, he looked out and found that, since his trip, every tree and blade of grass on the planet had disappeared.

(Ray Bradbury)

Some of the tiny actions in your life can magnify exponentially and create massive ripples in the lives of millions of people. How could Monica Lewinsky have possibly imagined the consequences of her flirting with Bill Clinton late in 1994?

As well as the upheaval created in the lives of the people who were directly involved, these actions have also been credited with leading to results as wide-ranging as stockmarket plunges around the globe, and even wars in the Middle East. This in turn would have created billions of other consequences... all from a series of actions lasting just a few seconds.

If there is light in the soul
    There will be beauty in the person.
If there is beauty in the person,
    There will be harmony in the house.
If there is harmony in the house,
    There will be order in the nation.
If there is order in the nation,
    There will be peace in the world.

                              (Chinese proverb)

If it were possible to calculate just how your ripples spread out from a single action, you may discover that you have accomplished similar results. I once accidentally overheard part of a conversation at a business breakfast, and it eventually resulted in my travelling halfway around the world, making many new friends, and discovering an entirely different perspective on my work.

I have since shared that new work perspective with thousands of other people. Many later told me how these ideas have altered their own work and family life, and it all began with the brief conversation I overheard.

So that you can determine how the ripple effect has operated in your own life, begin with some key aspect of your life at present, and thus work backwards until you remember perhaps a single action that set the ripples moving.

For instance, how did you form a certain relationship? Why are you working where you are now? What encouraged you to begin with a sport you play, or with a hobby you pursue? When I ask people to do this activity, they are often astonished how insignificant the action was that sowed the seed for a change in direction.

To change the world for the better does not necessarily take massive effort, or lots of money, or political power. Planetary change can come from those tiny things that we each do every day. It just needs you, me and everyone else to believe that our regular everyday activities can make that special difference.

The Ripple Effect

A man was once busy building a home for himself. He wanted it to be the nicest, cosiest home in the world. Someone came to him for help because the world was on fire, but it was his home he was interested in, not the world. When he finally finished his home, he found he did not have a planet to put it on.

(Anthony de Mello)

---

2. Everything is connected

In the early 1950s, the island of Borneo was ravaged by a malaria plague. The World Health Organisation (WHO) duly sprayed the entire island with DDT to eradicate the mosquitoes carrying the disease. The spraying was successful, and the incidence of malaria dropped.

However, soon after, the thatched roofs of the islanders' huts began collapsing, because the DDT had also killed the wasps that ate thatch-eating caterpillars, allowing the caterpillars to multiply.

The DDT also built up through the food chain, from insects, to lizards, and even to cats. As the cats died out, the rat population increased. The rats then created an outbreak of sylvatic plague and typhus, and the WHO finally had to parachute live cats into Borneo to redress the imbalance.

(Corinne McLaughlin & Gordon Davidson)

In everyday life, we find that nothing can ever occur in isolation. As an example, law enforcement agencies are often hampered by these interconnections. When a massive drug shipment is intercepted, authorities quite rightly feel proud of their efforts. Unfortunately, it can often inadvertently create a crime wave soon after.

Because the drugs are removed from the open market, the price of that drug eventually increases due to the limited supply, and addicts then commit more crime to pay the higher price.

The Ripple Effect

> *When we try to pick out anything by itself, we find it hitched to everything else in the universe.*
>
> *(John Muir)*

These complex interconnections are also demonstrated by the scientific concept of entrainment, which explains how similar life forms have a collective consciousness, and can act as a single entity.

For instance, when people participate in choirs and music bands, many of their vital body functions perform at similar rates. This includes their breathing patterns, their heart rates, and even their brain wave patterns.

This connectedness can be sensed by the individuals in the group. If you have ever sung in a choir, or played an instrument in a band, you may be familiar with this feeling.

In other examples of entrainment, large flocks of birds, flying in unison, will flick and change direction as one. Women in prisons and college dormitories will often find that their menstrual cycles fall into alignment. Giant schools of fish will swim as one, flicking and turning as if they are a single entity.

Everything is intricately connected to everything else. It is as though all life on Earth is part of a magical spider's web. When you touch one part, it can set off vibrations in many other parts, thereby causing a ripple effect.

The science of ecology teaches us that everything in the universe is connected. We cannot separate ourselves from the consequences of even the least of our actions: Whatever we do <u>here</u> comes back <u>there</u>.

(Eknath Easwaran)

3. What goes around comes around

At the personal level

A friend of mine once worked for a ruthless boss who frequently harangued his office staff for little or no reason. This led to a higher turnover of disgruntled employees, which meant that the boss then had to work many extra hours to arrange the paperwork and retraining of the new workers.

This boss's professional life demonstrated that what goes around comes around. Because all life events are so interconnected, any action you take here will eventually come back to affect you there. As you sow, so shall you reap.

Your life resembles a boomerang, in which the consequences of your actions will later return and influence you in some way. This places the ripples in a powerful light. Even if you choose to ignore the effect of your actions on others, those actions will nevertheless change your own life.

Let's look at some further examples of this boomerang effect:
- According to a much-loved urban myth (which doubtlessly has happened at some stage), a young man was once late for a job interview, yet he stopped to help an elderly woman change a flat tyre on her car. When he arrived for the interview, he discovered that the woman he assisted was the C.E.O. of the company he hoped to work for. She was present at the interview and, yes, he was eventually offered the job.

*If you help others, you will be helped,
perhaps tomorrow, perhaps in one
hundred years, but you will be helped.
Nature must pay off the debt.
It is a mathematical law and
all life is mathematics.*

(Gurdjieff)

- Several years ago, a violent storm was approaching a small town in the United States. The radio report warned that power could be blacked out for some time, and that residents should stock up on necessary supplies. One resident, however, rushed to the local store, and bought much more than he would possibly need. A little later, other residents in desperate need of basic supplies were unable to buy them because of their selfish neighbour.

During the storm, several houses were unroofed, including the roof of the selfish resident. After the storm had passed, he discovered that few of his neighbours were willing to offer assistance in any way.

At the corporate level

Large groups and organisations also discover that what goes around comes around. With the implementation of economic rationalist philosophy in the past ten years, many companies have cut costs at every opportunity. Yet, at a later date, these same companies have sometimes found that their expenses became much higher because of the strategies they earlier applied to cut their expenditure.

Examples include:
- Only one-third of organisations that downsize their staff improve their profit margin at a later date. The staff who remain are often overworked, as they are required to do part of the work of those who were fired. They are also tense and distrusting, wondering who will next be asked to leave. Such factors are not very conducive to effective work, and thus the initial downsizing often leads to less productive results for the organisation.

*We cannot live only for ourselves.
A thousand fibres connect us with our
fellow men; and among those fibres,
as sympathetic threads, our actions
run as causes, and they come
back to us as effects.*

(Herman Melville)

- In a country town, a hardware store continually forced a local supplier to offer a lower price for their products. However, because their margins were too narrow, the local supplier eventually went bankrupt. The hardware store then had to find another more expensive supplier in the nearest capital city, which ended up costing them far more than the original supplier was charging them.
- In Victoria, the Railway Department replaced many of the station ticket-sellers with automatic ticket machines. It was projected that the savings on wages would be considerable. However, vandals discovered that, by pouring a certain type of acid into the unsupervised machines, they could empty the money stored inside. Expensive security guards then were hired to patrol the railway stations. The final cost was far in excess of maintaining the original ticket-sellers at the stations.

The Ripple Effect

> *I believe a leaf of grass is
> no less than the journey-
> work of the stars.*
>
> *(Walt Whitman)*

Key points about the ripple effect

To understand how our beautiful planet functions each day, take all of the examples offered so far, and multiply them six-billion-fold. To many people, this just sounds too overwhelming, so let's clarify some basic principles that may make it easier to comprehend the ripple effect.

- **The effect** of your initial input is not proportional to the effect of the resulting ripples. A small seemingly inconsequential action, such as smiling at a stranger, can magnify exponentially and create a major future event. Conversely, an event that initially appears significant, such as a presidential visit, may later cause only minor flurries.

- **Ripples move** outwards in chaotic three-dimensional circles, and not necessarily in neat linear forms. The world's daily events are often too complex to be considered only in a simplistic cause-and-effect chain. Although many of the anecdotes in this book are *chain* stories (if you do *this*, then eventually *that* will happen), they still represent just a thin slice of an overall picture involving perhaps millions of events. To view the ripples at work fully, you would need a wide-angle camera, not a telephoto lens.

- **Once your** ripples spread further afield, they can interconnect with those released by many other people, eventually to create a single consequence. While just one action may be the chief cause of a specific result, that result may also have been from the convergence of thousands of earlier actions. Many events on this planet occur because of the sum total of the ripples that join together at that particular time.

The Ripple Effect

> To see the world in a grain of sand
>
> and heaven in a wild flower
>
> hold infinity in the palm of your hand
>
> and eternity in an hour.
>
> (William Blake)

- **Ripples can** be created by what you do, and also by what you don't do. Naturally, any action that you take will possibly cause other things to happen. However, *not* taking an action can also lead to other consequences that may otherwise not have occurred. If you neglect to warn someone of some dangerous stairs, they may fall and break a leg.

- **It is the** cumulative total of millions of daily events from all of us that often change the world. If just 5 per cent of a city's population decide to take one less drive to work each week, the decreased incidence of air pollution in the area is significantly less, and easily measurable.

- **Ripples are** enhanced by modern technology. The Internet has become a worldwide electronic web, on which connections can be made around the globe in an instant. Thus, an e-mail written in the United States can cause an immediate positive reaction in fifty different countries. Throughout history, many have believed that we are One, that all people are spiritually interconnected. Our technology is now creating an artificial version of this One-ness.

We must become the change

we seek in the world.

(Gandhi)

SPREADING THE RIPPLES:
Ideas for making a difference to the world every day

So you would like to make a positive difference to the world? Then it is important that you focus on two special forms of *work* in your life.

ONE. The first is your inner work, which involves the daily practice, analysis and ongoing learning that enables you to reach for your God-given potential.

This inner work should focus on your physical, emotional, spiritual and mental development. Such work is necessary if you wish to spread inspiring ripples.

This is because the key to creating change around you is to first create the change *in* you.

For example, if you believe that people should be more loving and tolerant, then you must show them how by being more loving and tolerant in your own life.

Personal actions speak much louder than advice directed at others. It is your actions that are more likely to spread ripples in the lives of those around you.

When you bought this book, perhaps you had hoped that it would offer ideas on how you could change the rest of the world. Unfortunately, unless you focus on your inner work, you are much less likely to create positive ripples in the lives of others.

What an illusion to think you can change the world without having first changed yourself.

(Carl Jung)

TWO. The second is your outer work, which occurs whenever you volunteer your labour, or assist members of your own family, or interact with another person in an affirming way.

To offer support to people around you in this way is the price you pay for being allowed to live on this planet.

It is during these countless communications every day that you make your special difference to the world, at first in an immediate sense, and eventually through the ripples that spread ever outwards.

Much of the quality of this outer work will be determined by the efforts you have made with your inner work.

In the following pages, you will be offered many ideas for making a difference in the lives of other people. These ideas will combine the concepts of your inner and your outer work.

I will act as if what I do makes a difference.

(William James)

You can make a difference to the world if you:

Take personal responsibility   **1**

> **People who accept responsibility for what they do take ownership of their actions, and those actions then are more likely to contribute positive benefits to the world.**

Have you ever looked for a **scapegoat** *when something goes wrong in your life? This is when you search for someone or something else that you can blame for the problem. The term* **scapegoat** *comes from the Book of Leviticus in the Old Testament, and relates to a custom known as the* **escaped goat**.

Over 4000 years ago, in times of trouble, the people would take a healthy goat to the temple. The high priest would then place his hands on the goat's head and announce all of the people's problems and miseries. Once these woes had been transferred to the goat, it would be set free, thus becoming an **escaped goat**, *and taking the people's troubles with it.*

Some things have not changed very much in the past 4000 years. We are still looking for scapegoats for our problems, rather than taking responsibility for them ourselves.

For example, in the past few years, some of the libel cases in the Western world have made a laughing stock of the present legal system. People have sued restaurants for providing hot coffee which they then spilt on their own lap, or holiday resorts because they slipped on soap in the shower. There surely must be a limit to blaming someone else for troubles that we have caused ourselves.

If you would like to know the effect choices have on one's life, look at yourself — what you see is the choices you've made.

(Shad Helmstetter)

It is all very well to insist on your rights in life (including your right to take legal action when it is warranted), but this must be balanced with taking personal responsibility for your actions. Unfortunately, some people seem to have forgotten about being responsible for what they do.

They are so convinced they are the victim that they immediately look for a scapegoat, for someone *out there* who is at fault. If this trend continues, we will end up creating a rights-obsessed, rather than responsibility-driven, civilisation.

This is why ripples thinking is so necessary today. It helps you to believe that you can make a difference, which then can give you the confidence to take responsibility for your actions. It is when you ask: "What can I do about this?" rather than "Who can I blame for this?" It means that you can be part of the solution, and not part of the problem.

Ripples thinking is not about making you feel guilty about everything you do, or forcing you to feel responsible for every misery on the planet. It is about believing in your own positive efforts to resolve an issue whenever you can, and focusing your energy on what you can do, not on what others might be doing to you.

Genuine change in the world then comes from what you attend to every day. One less trip in your own car. One extra donation to a worthwhile charity. One positive word to a colleague. Responsible people such as you can make a small but vital difference to the quality of life on this planet.

The Ripple Effect

> *I don't know what your destiny will be, but one thing I do know: the only ones among you who will be really happy are those who have sought and found how to serve.*
>
> *(Albert Schweitzer)*

You can make a difference to the world if you:

Do volunteer work

> When you do volunteer work for those in need, you have a direct influence in their lives.

Volunteer work has two superb benefits. The first is that the needy recipients enjoy the benefits of the work that you do. The second benefit is that it is great for your physical, mental and spiritual health.

Volunteers often comment on what is called helper's high, in which they experience immediate feel-good sensations such as heightened energy and a wonderful inner warmth. Thus, to consciously apply the ripple effect through your volunteer work can in fact be beneficial for you as well as for the people you help.

If you would like to discover this helper's high, perhaps you could deliver meals to aged people, or volunteer to teach adult reading classes. Maybe you would like to spend some time each week working in a charity clothing store, or helping out with some reading groups at your local infants school.

When is the last time that you gave some volunteer help? This is not meant to make you feel guilty, but it must be remembered that many community groups would collapse without the support of their volunteers. These groups are often the lifeblood of the local area, and provide services that cannot always be afforded by government organisations.

> *When a lot of people do a little, it's a lot. When a lot of people do nothing — it's nothing.*
>
> *(Harvey Diamond)*

Volunteer work can also be carried out at the corporate level. For instance, why not encourage your company to allow each employee to volunteer one day's service a month to a local community organisation? This service would be provided on a regular workday, with the employee being paid by the company. The multiple benefits would include:

- increased assistance for the community group
- positive reinforcement of your company as a fully contributing community member
- employees who feel re-energised by doing something different each month.

Australian bank Westpac offers many similar services through its staff volunteering program. Over one-third of its staff are directly involved as local community volunteers. They are offered paid time off work, and flexible work arrangements, to enable them to meet these community commitments.

Westpac will also match, dollar for dollar, any contributions that a staff member contributes to a tax deductible charity. Many other major corporations throughout Australia offer similar programs. Such initiatives show clearly that the community spirit is alive and well in the corporate world.

There are many possibilities for offering volunteer work. Whether you act in an individual capacity, or with a group of inspired people in your workplace, the opportunities are only limited by your imagination.

Remember that volunteer work is one of the most direct ways of spreading ripples to other people in need. The opportunity is immediate, the structures for helping others often are already in place.

*A bit of fragrance always clings
to the hand that gives you roses.
(Chinese proverb)*

For a special example of the volunteer spirit, look no further than the Jewish legend known as lamed-vov. *According to this tradition, there are always thirty-six people alive in the world who selflessly contribute their services for those around them (*lamed-vov *means thirty-six).*

These thirty-six people may be famous, unknown, rich, or poor, but they are genuine and caring human beings who always look for ways that they can help others. They do not know that they are one of the lamed-vov, *and anyone who claims that they are a* lamed-vov *is not.*

Lamed-vov *can often be found in local church groups, charity organisations and other community committees, selflessly contributing their time and effort to making the world a better place for others. It might even be someone you know. In fact, who in your own life do you believe would be a* lamed-vov?

Consumerism in the Western nations will never be changed or reduced by asking people to stop consuming. It will change only when people are inspired by a more noble, worthy and fulfilling purpose for their lives. This purpose could be described as the spiritual growth and mutual empowerment of all people in the world.
(McLaughlan & Davidson)

You can make a difference to the world if you:

Purchase wisely (3)

> **When you purchase a product or make an investment, you set off many ripples that can create positive or negative consequences.**

Money talks. When you buy a product or a service, you spread powerful ripples. Your payment gives a specific message to the suppliers about your personal preferences and acceptance of their products. You are indicating that you support most, if not all, aspects of their operation.

If you purchase some running shoes from a company that exploits child slave labour in third world countries, and you are aware of this fact, then you are tacitly agreeing with this exploitation.

If your investments are placed with a company that pursues unethical practices, and you know about those practices, then you are virtually signalling approval for those operations. To invest with such groups can compromise your own ethics.

You have the power to register your disapproval at what they do. Simply refuse to give them your money. Make your protest in a small but significant way. If a multinational corporation despoils the environment, or abuses the rights of indigenous people in poor countries, then don't invest in their products.

On the other hand, if a company pursues a highly ethical stance with their operation, then show them that you support their beliefs by purchasing their products or investing in their shares.

> *There must be more to life than having everything!*
>
> *(Maurice Sendak)*

If your investments are controlled by financial managers, then check to see where they have specifically placed your money. If at all possible, ensure that it has been directed towards companies that align with your own set of ethics.

Until now, the factors that determined your choice of product have included value for money, product reputation, quality of service, and product durability. An extra reason should now be taken into account when you make a purchase or an investment.

This extra vital factor is to consider the ripples you create if you purchase the product.

From now on, pause for just a second before committing your money, and think about the messages of support you are giving by making that investment. Because of your purchase, you can set off many positive or negative ripples that create consequences in endless ways.

On average, a consumer in a Western nation will purchase at least 5000 items or services each year. Some people will acquire double that number. This will include their grocery shopping, gift purchases, payments for services and an endless array of incidental transactions. Every single one of these transactions, without exception, is creating ripples for the provider, the manufacturer and many other people involved in the provision of that item or service.

The Ripple Effect

> *A man never discloses his own character so clearly as when he describes another's.*
> *(Jean Paul Friedrich Richter)*

You can make a difference to the world if you:

Watch what you say

Ripples are spread every day by *word-of-mouth* in regular conversations.

The human grapevine is one of the clearest examples of the ripple effect in everyday action. A passing comment from you, spoken in just a few seconds, could eventually change someone's life. A single piece of gossip, begun by one person, can spread like wildfire through an entire city within a few hours.

Even on this very day, there are reputations being made and broken by *word-of-mouth* all around the world. Reputation is a fragile concept, and one malicious rumour spread by a single person can destroy credibility that may have taken years to develop. Businesses, for instance, can thrive or fail because of such gossiping.

Just recently, a top-quality restaurant in my local area was crippled by a rumour that a customer had suffered food poisoning after eating there. Bookings dropped dramatically in the next few weeks, yet the restaurant owner was able later to prove that the story was simply not true.

Whenever you take part in a conversation, you should be aware of the consequences of what is being said. It is no exaggeration to state that one slip of the tongue can ruin someone's life. Thus, if someone secretively tells you something that you suspect is not true, you should make an effort to stop the gossip spreading any further.

There is a great man, who makes every man feel small. But the real great man is the man who makes every man feel great.
(G. K. Chesterton)

Ask them how they would feel if a similar rumour was being told about them. Remind them of the ripple effect they create every time they take part in spreading innuendo about others.

Naturally, there are positive forms of gossip on the human grapevine as well, and you should indulge in them whenever you can. Spread stories about the good actions of others, especially when they are not present at the time.

I once worked with a woman who continually told us about the great work that she had seen others doing. She was a wonderful example of someone who spread positive ripples at every opportunity.

You will give yourself peace
of mind if you do every act
as if it were your last.
(Marcus Aurelius)

You can make a difference to the world if you:

Make every action count (5)

Ripples can begin from any single thing that you do. Thus, you must treat every action as though it is the special one that will create lasting and purposeful change.

A young woman was walking along a deserted beach at sunset when, in the distance, she noticed an old man who kept leaning down, picking something up and throwing it out into the water. As she moved closer, she saw that the old man was picking up starfish that had been washed up on the beach and, one at a time, he was throwing them back into the water.

The woman was quite puzzled, so she walked up and said, "Good evening. Look, forgive me for intruding, but I was just wondering what you were doing?"

"Oh, I'm throwing starfish back into the water," replied the old man. "You see, it's high tide right now and all of these starfish have been washed up onto the shore. If I don't throw them back, they'll die up here."

"I understand," she responded, "but there must be thousands of starfish on this beach. You can't get to all of them. There are too many. And don't you realise this is probably happening on hundreds of beaches all up and down the coast? Can't you see that you can't possibly make a difference?"

The old man smiled, bent down and picked up yet another starfish. And as he threw it back into the sea, he replied, "Made a difference to that one!"

Somebody should tell us right from the start that we are dying. Then we might live life to the limit — every minute of every day.

Do it, I say. Whatever you want to do, do it now!

There are only so many tomorrows.

(Michael Landon)

Treasure every single human action. With each tiny effort, you may be planting a positive seed that could grow forever. Just imagine. It may be your very next action.

Even while you are reading this book, your phone may ring, and a close friend may be asking for support. You may be interrupted by a child who is standing beside you, and is asking you to play a game. Right there, at that moment it is a starting point for the ripple effect.

This is why it is so important that you focus on every single thing that you do as you interact with other people, because that very next action could have infinite consequences. Ensure that your actions count, because this is how you make a difference to the world.

Consider the power of these everyday actions from the perspective of your own life. Are there any occasions when a brief experience, a chance meeting, a passing comment, has set you off in a different direction and created an expanding multitude of effects?

Perhaps you spent a few seconds talking to a stranger at a party, who mentioned a job opportunity about to become available at his company. You later apply for, and receive, this new position.

Within your first week at work, you meet your partner-in-life, and become married within a year. This work also leads to a chance meeting with a long-lost friend during a business meeting.

All of these changes in your life may have resulted from the way that you presented yourself to that stranger at the party. Your brief smile, and positive greeting, may have been enough to encourage them to tell you about that job opportunity.

The Ripple Effect

> *In a world where death is the hunter,*
> *my friend, there is no time for regrets or*
> *doubts. There is only time for decisions.*
> *(Carlos Castaneda)*

Thus, great changes in your life may have come from those few tiny actions. Naturally, to calculate the consequences for everything you do in your life would be impossible. Nevertheless, it is important to make every action count.

Remember that genuine change on Earth does not come only from spectacular major events that are sensationalised in the world media. In many cases, lasting change comes from the countless tiny things that each of us does every day.

The events covered by the media are only the tiniest fraction of everything that happens on the planet that day. Out of a total of trillions of events, your TV news may cover perhaps twenty.

The vast majority of actions are the everyday ones in which you, me and everyone else participate. These are the worthy efforts that really change the world. And your individual greatness lies in how you perform those small but significant things on a regular basis. This includes your very next action. Make it count. It might change someone's life.

Listening requires more intelligence than speaking.

(Turkish proverb)

You can make a difference to the world if you:

Really listen to others (6)

> **When you listen fully to someone, you are more likely to find out what they need. You will then be able to help them more effectively.**

A woman seeking a divorce went to visit her lawyer. The first question he asked was: "Do you have grounds for divorce?" "Yes," she replied. "About two hectares."

"Perhaps I'm not making myself clear," he said. "Do you have a grudge?" "No, but we have a carport," she responded.

"Let me try again. Does your husband beat you up?" he said impatiently. "Yes, generally he gets up before I do," she said.

At this point, the lawyer decided to try a different tack. "Ma'am, are you sure you really want a divorce?"

"Well, I don't want one at all," she said. "But my husband does. He claims we have difficulty communicating."

(Pat Swindall)

Listening is one of our most important social skills, yet it is becoming increasingly neglected by modern society. Rapid-fire conversation is characterised by the short sharp retorts that feature on the 30-minute T.V. sitcom shows.

In such situations, the emphasis is placed on the fast-paced wit of the speaker, rather than on the quality of the listening taking place.

> *Am I the bulb or the light?*
>
> *(Joseph Campbell)*

Partly because of role-models such as these, people are taking less time to listen well. They are also conditioned into doing so by the 5-second media bites that feature on the news and in advertisements. Such an approach is too often carried over into everyday life.

Listen to those around you, and you will constantly hear people who interrupt others halfway through what they were saying. They just do not take the time to listen deeply and thoughtfully.

Although we were all given two ears and one mouth at birth, some people seem to act as if the ratio is the other way around in their everyday lives.

Excellent listeners are often the ones who are most capable of spreading effective ripples. By listening closely, they are more likely to find out what is needed by the speaker, and thus are more able to help them.

One special example of this is Lifeline Australia's telephone crisis line. In many cases, the counsellors simply listen to the caller. Yet it has been demonstrated that these single calls can positively alter the caller's life.

Genuine listeners also learn more about life. After all, if you do all the talking, you will only reinforce what you already know. When you listen to others, you benefit from their knowledge and experience.

Hearing the ideas shared by different people gives you the opportunity to act upon those ideas, and thus to spread ripples in the lives of others.

*Our deepest fear is not that we are inadequate. Our deepest fear is that we are powerful beyond measure. It is our light, not our darkness, that most frightens us. We ask ourselves, who am I to be brilliant, gorgeous, talented and fabulous? Actually, who are you **not** to be?*
(Nelson Mandela)

You can make a difference to the world if you:

Believe in your own talents

> **Powerful ripples are created by those who believe in their talents, and are prepared to live up to the potential of those talents.**

Throughout his life, Renoir was told by many people that he had no talent, and that he should give up with his painting. An art expert once looked at some of Renoir's work, and sneered: "You are, I presume, dabbling in painting to amuse yourself." To this, Renoir replied: "Of course. When it ceases to amuse me, I will stop painting."

Near the end of his life, Renoir suffered from advanced rheumatism in his hands. This caused him considerable pain with every brushstroke he took. Upon seeing this, Matisse asked him: "Why is it that you still have to work? Why do you continue to push yourself?" To which Renoir answered: "The pain passes, but the pleasure, the creation of beauty, remains."

When you believe in your own talents, you can create daily changes all around you. Renoir refused to give up on his belief in his talent, and even today, his work continues to generate ripples in the hearts and minds of millions of people.

Have you ever wondered why you have been placed on Earth in this lifetime? Here is one possibility. You are here to live up to your God-given potential, to make the most of whatever talents you were given at birth and through your life thus far. You may have a talent for organising finances, or making friends, or growing beautiful gardens.

Use what talent you possess. The woods would be very silent if no bird sang except those that sang the very best.

(Henry Van Dyke)

Whatever your talents, it is up to you to do the absolute best that you can to develop it. When you do this, the ripples from your actions will naturally be more effective because you will be doing what you are best at doing. However, if you fail to make the most of your talent, you will not only let yourself down, but also the many others who would have benefited from your efforts.

Admittedly, it may not always be easy to display your talents freely and openly. You will occasionally meet people who have become consumed with average-ness, and with demeaning those who aspire to exceptional standards. Sadly, this is a reflection upon their own standards.

But you must not let their insecurities weigh you down. You can respond simply by displaying your talent on every occasion it is appropriate to do so.

To put that talent into practice, learn to set goals in your life. Only 3 per cent of people consistently place their goals on paper when it is appropriate to do so. These people are far more likely to attain their goals, to make them a reality.

Talented people who achieve special goals in life do two things well. The first is that they clearly visualise their goals, mentally rehearsing the end-result over and over in their mind. The second is that they persevere with the many tiny steps needed to put the goal into place.

If you wish to make a special difference to the world, then you must believe in your talents, and be prepared to place those talents into action by setting specific goals. There is little sense in only offering a pale imitation of your true self to others. Powerful ripples come from those who open the gifts they were given at birth.

> *Put your heart, mind, intellect and soul even to your smallest acts. This is the secret of success.*
>
> *(Swami Swanada)*

You can make a difference to the world if you:

Reflect on your actions

> **When you reflect upon your daily life, your energies will become more focused, and your capacity for creating powerful ripples will be enhanced.**

Our lives are like the tide, going in and out every day. It is a law of nature to create a balance between the ebb and flow in all energy cycles, and so it should be with our own lives. As the tide comes in, we devote our energy to the labours of our life. As it goes out again, we take a rest, and revive ourselves for the next wave of action.

Can you imagine what would happen if the tide kept coming in, and in, and in? Coastal areas would soon be inundated. Have you noticed what happens when you keep working, and working, and working, without pausing to reflect on the effectiveness of your actions? You can feel flooded by life.

So you must let the tide go out again. It gives you the opportunity to adjust and improve upon your efforts.

One of the most powerful ways of letting the tide out is to consciously reflect on your actions as often as possible. This means that you must take the time to stop, to think, and to then act upon some of those reflections.

Admittedly, this advice contradicts some present-day work practices that are based upon relentless energy-draining labour.

We must cultivate our garden.

(Voltaire)

However, if you can manage to balance your hard work with some time for reflection, you will have more energy to give to what you do. Your ripples will be more effective, and will be more likely to make a positive difference for others.

One special way to develop some reflective practice in your life is to write out your thoughts regularly in a journal. Purchase a small hardcover booklet, and set aside several times each week to reflect on your daily efforts. The format of your entries is entirely up to you. Some people prefer to jot down their thoughts as they occur at the time.

One option is to write your responses to questions such as "What went well today?" and "How could I have done things differently?" It is worthwhile to include the date of these entries, so that you can re-read your thoughts at a later time. Perhaps you also could write about the positive ripples that you believe you have created that day.

In Japanese society, a worker who is thinking, pondering or reflecting quietly will often be left alone. It will be assumed that the worker is fulfilling a worthwhile function. In most Western cultures, however, when someone is reflecting, it is assumed that they can be interrupted. To be sitting and thinking quietly is generally not considered to be a productive activity.

No one ever hurt their eyesight by looking at the bright side of life.

(Anon)

You can make a difference to the world if you:

Look for the good in others (9)

When you look for the good in others, you support the kinds of actions that make a positive contribution to the world.

Throughout your life, you will find what you are looking for. For instance, if you search for what is negative in the people you meet, you will probably be successful. It is not a perfect world. With sufficient effort, you will manage to find something that is *wrong* with most people. Conversely, if you look for the good in others, you are also likely to find it.

A wise old man was once sitting beside the road. He was asked for advice by two travellers. The first traveller said: "Old man, in the town up ahead, what are the people like?"

The old man said: "What did you think of the people in the last town?"

"I found them to be rude and ignorant."

"Then you will find those in the next town to be the same."

Some time later, the second traveller happened upon the same spot and asked: "Old man, in the town up ahead, what are the people like?"

And the old man said: "What did you think of the people in the last town?"

"I found them to be friendly and positive."

"Then you will find those in the next town to be the same."

The greatest of all human potentials is the potential of each one of us to empower and acknowledge the other.

(Jean Houston)

When you make the effort to see the essential moral goodness in others, you will soon discover what is called the self-fulfilling prophecy. People you meet will act in just the way that you expect them to.

This prophecy plays a powerful role in the interactions of parents and teachers with children in their care. For instance, if you are convinced that a child is going to misbehave, he or she will usually live down to your expectations.

You will then react according to your negative beliefs about that child, and perhaps say something like: "That's the sort of poor behaviour I expected from you."

However, if you are convinced of the child's essential goodness, your positive response to their behaviour will indicate this. You will invariably reinforce the good that they do, simply because it is what you expected from them.

In such situations, you should offer verbal feedback on their efforts. This reinforces their positive actions, and can encourage them to attempt further efforts.

Think of a time when someone gave supportive feedback to you. Do you remember how such recognition inspired you to continue with your efforts?

My wife Sharon lives her life according to this perspective. Sharon manages to find something good in virtually everyone she meets, and invariably tells them about it. Not surprisingly, all of these people hold her in high regard.

To see things in the seed,

that is genius.

(Lao-tzu)

Is it any wonder? Most of us would like to think that we too have an essential goodness in ourselves, and so we are attracted to those who recognise our positive features.

People who look for the good in others are creating powerful ripples every time they interact with another person. They are reminding us of what is good in the world, and encouraging us to follow their example.

Imagination is more important than knowledge.

(Albert Einstein)

You can make a difference to the world if you:

Create new ideas

> A single creative thought can lead to a new product or practice that may eventually change your life, as well as the lives of many other people.

Johannes Gutenberg developed the printing press by combining two previously unconnected devices, the coin punch and the wine press. Coin punches had been used to make an image on small objects such as gold coins, while the wine press had squeezed juice out of grapes by applying force to a wide area.

In a creative moment, Gutenberg took a bunch of coin punches and put them under the force of the wine press so that they left their images on paper. The printing press had been invented.

The human brain is the most phenomenal entity in the known world. It is one hundred billion neurons dancing to a universal song. It is the creator of your reality in every moment of your life.

At one time or another, someone's brain has been responsible for every new idea that has ever been created on our planet. And every time one of these new ideas is released for others, it sets off ripples that change the world forever.

Witness the famous inventions throughout our history that have enriched our way of living, such as the printing press, electricity, the telephone and the computer. From the time they were offered to the general public, they made a tangible difference in the lives of millions of people.

What if you slept?
And what if,
in your sleep
you dreamed?
And what if,
in your dream,
you went to heaven
and there plucked
a strange and
beautiful flower?
And what if,
when you awoke,
you had the flower
in your hand?
(Samuel Taylor Coleridge)

If you wish to generate positive ripples with your own intellect, then here are a few exercises that may help you to create some innovative ideas:

- Every day, ask key questions such as "Why?" and "What if?" When you seek answers around you, your thinking is stimulated to consider alternatives. If you neglect to ask these questions, you may be accepting everything just as it is.
- Put yourself in someone else's shoes. See the world from their perspective. If nothing else, this can sometimes resolve arguments. Even pretend to be something else, such as a traffic light, a washing machine or a flower. Imagine what it would feel like to be that object throughout the year.
- Consciously exercise your intellect by brainstorming every day. Many people exercise their bodies, yet neglect their brain. To begin, you could generate a list of ridiculous and revolutionary ideas on topics such as how to lower the number of cars on the road, or how to eliminate world hunger.
- Set out to predict the future. Ponder how things will be in two, five or one hundred years from now. How will we travel around? Will everything really be done in virtual reality? What will clothing fashion be like? What new foods will we eat? Will there be a post-human society?

If your compassion does not include yourself, it is incomplete.

(Jack Kornfield)

You can make a difference to the world if you:

Look after yourself

> You are your own greatest asset. Look after yourself so that you will have the energy to make a difference in the lives of others.

When you climb onto a plane, a flight attendant will read out a safety warning, explaining how to use an oxygen mask in the event of an air pressure drop in the cabin. Near the end of the announcement, the attendant will then add: "And if you have children with you, then please place on your own mask first."

There is a powerful message here for anyone who is responsible for helping other people. You must look after yourself *as well as* helping everyone else.

If you constantly give your attention to others, rather than yourself, you will eventually burn out. The end result? You will be less likely to spread positive ripples to these people around you.

At first, this message seems to contradict the concept of the ripples. Surely, you may ask, you should help others at every opportunity? Yes, you should, but you must also make sure that you have the inner energy to do so.

This refers to parents, managers, teachers, nurses, social workers, and anyone else who is often exhausted from caring for people around them. Admittedly, it is a wonderful virtue to support others, but you won't be able to do so if you have run out of energy yourself.

The Ripple Effect

The privilege of a lifetime

is being who you are.

(Joseph Campbell)

It is not a selfish act to look after yourself first. In fact, it is entirely admirable. It only becomes selfish if you later refuse to offer help to others.

You must see yourself as your greatest asset. Some people look after their houses and their cars better than their own bodies and minds. Yet, if they fail to nurture themselves, they will eventually lose both their houses and their cars, not to mention their health and vitality.

Become the president of your own fan club. Treat yourself as though you are your own favourite person. And with the energy you create within your own body, mind and soul, you will then be more capable of spreading ripples in the world around you.

People touch our lives, if only for a moment; and yet we're not the same, from that moment on. The time is not important: the moment is forever.

(Fern Bork)

You can make a difference to the world if you:

Write encouraging messages

> Powerful ripples can be created when you send a written message to other people. However, you must choose those words with care, because they will exist for all eternity.

If you ever wish to convince someone of the ripple effect, then remind them of the last chain letter that they received. Whether these letters are positive (tell five other people about the good work they do) or negative (send money to the last five addresses on this note), it does not take long for the message to spread far and wide.

If each receiver sends the note to another five people, in a very short space of time, over one million recipients will have received the same message. Intriguingly, the negative ones (those that ask for money) quickly break down, with only the first few gaining a benefit from the chain letter. However, the positive ones could continue indefinitely, perhaps until every person on the planet has received a copy of the letter.

In your everyday life, ripples can spread from written messages just as powerfully as they do from verbal and eye-to-eye contacts that you make with others. These written messages can include letters, faxes, cards or e-mail.

On the private level, they may involve the greetings that you send to close friends, lovers and relatives, notes that could be forever treasured. At a community level, they may include the letters that you post to the media, or to key people who are responsible for making significant changes in your local community.

Just as a drop of water causes ripples in a pond, so a thought dropped into the pool of consciousness can cause ever-expanding ripples in the universal human mind.
(Jean Richards)

Remember that what you place in writing is a permanent record. It will be there forever. On the other hand, a verbal comment is short-lived and may be easily forgotten. On paper, or on screen, a written message is a commitment for all eternity. Thus, give some thought to the words before you write them. Once sent, there can be no turning back.

Whenever possible, look for the good things that have been done, and let the recipient of your message know about it. There are already enough people around who delight in looking for what's wrong with something, and then telling the rest of us about it.

Associating with such people will only lower your energy level. Most letters sent to newspaper editors are critical of someone's actions or beliefs, yet they could just as easily offer praise for the efforts of others.

If you are going to write something on a particular day, then send notes that will make an inspiring difference in the life of the recipient.

Several years ago, I was approached by a woman who attended one of my talks. She asked if I could send her some professional material. Happy to oblige, I later posted this material, and included an extra note with some upbeat comments on how she could make the most of her day.

Two years later, I chanced to meet her at a shopping centre. She proceeded to tell me that my letter had arrived on a day when her whole life had virtually fallen apart, and it was only the positive energy of my words that had held her together.

The best portions of a good man's life,

    His little, nameless, unremembered acts,

Of kindness and love.

                  (William Wordsworth)

Even now, she said, the note was still in her possession, and she would occasionally take it out and read it to boost her morale.

I thanked the stars that I had made the effort to write that note in the first place. Obviously, the ripples that had spread from my few minutes of writing had made a difference in someone's life.

There is more to life

than increasing its speed.

(Gandhi)

You can make a difference to the world if you:

Find your natural pace⑬

> When you discover your natural pace, it will give you the time and the energy to create more effective ripples in your life.

Accompanied by his full entourage, an African explorer in the nineteenth century was marching relentlessly through the jungle towards a distant mountain. In his haste to reach his destination, he was using every means possible to force his native bearers to go faster. Threats, beatings and promises rained down incessantly on the hardworking locals as they struggled through the heavy undergrowth.

However, as they neared the mountain, the bearers abruptly stopped and sat down. No amount of threats or even extra pay would induce them to stand and move on. And when asked why they would not continue, they simply replied, "Because we are waiting for our souls to catch up."

As the native bearers explained, you leave your soul behind when you go faster than your natural pace. You will recognise this in your life by a feeling of always being rushed for time. It is as though God is holding down the fast-forward button on the heavenly remote control, and pointing it directly at you.

Your natural pace is a rhythm of life that allows you to create your most inspiring and powerful ripples. Each person has a preferred pace, and it is important to align your everyday actions with this natural pace.

*It's not about lack of action.
It's about having action come
from a quiet place inside.*

(Ram Dass)

If you move faster than your individual pace, you will end up feeling consumed by the speed of modern-day life. On the other hand, if you are forced to move slower than your natural pace, you will probably find life to be lacking in stimulation.

Your pace can also change through your life. Most 20-year-olds prefer a different pace to 60-year-olds. As well, the boss may prefer a different pace to some of his or her employees. That is when we hear comments such as "She's just lazy" or "At the rate he works, he'll have a heart attack."

Your own pace may also seem like a mad rush to some, where as others may be convinced that you should be working much faster. In effect, we all have our own pace. So learn to respect others for the pace they prefer, but beware of speeding yourself up just to suit someone else.

To find your own pace, and thus spread more effective ripples, you will need to listen very carefully to your soul. Some of the following suggestions may help you in that cause:

- Stand in a place of natural beauty, such as a forest, or on a beach, and align yourself with the pace of the natural world around you. You may notice that it moves at a steady rate that is sustainable over millions of years. At the same time, humanity burns itself out by adopting three speeds, namely, fast, faster and fastest. So, observe that natural pace. Become a part of your surroundings for several hours at least. Slow yourself down to the natural world around you.

For what shall it profit a man,

if he shall gain the whole world,

and lose his own soul?

(Mark 8:36)

- Start your day by touching base with your soul. Early in the morning, ponder the great things that you intend to accomplish that day. Think about the wonderful consequences of some of the ripples that you could spread.
- For a few minutes at least, do everything more slowly. Pretend that you are in a slow-motion movie. When you do this, it gives you time to think about the things you are doing. Surprisingly, you might find that you accomplish more in this *slow time* than you normally do in your rushed time.
- Whenever possible, do one thing at a time. Focus on the task at hand. Don't do ten things at once. You might end up only half-completing many of those tasks. There is something very unsatisfying about failing to finish your projects in life. So do one thing properly before you move on to others.
- Consume what you need, rather than what you want. If you always want for more, your soul becomes unsettled by the accelerated pace necessary to acquire those goods and services. Material objects may be a part of life in the Western world, but there has to be a limit somewhere. Set your limits according to your soul's need, and not to your mind's greed.

A hundred years from now, it will not matter what my bank account was, the sort of house I lived in, or the kind of car I drove... but the world may be different because I was important in the life of a child.

(Anon)

You can make a difference to the world if you:

Focus on your own family

Before you set out to create change for the whole world, you should start by supporting the members of your own family.

In the United States at the turn of the millennium:
- *On average, children have less than a 50 per cent chance of growing up with both parents.*
- *More than 60 per cent of children need day care because of their parent's work demands.*
- *Juvenile violent crime is up 500 per cent from the 1950s.*
- *Each week, a school-age child spends 2 hours reading, and 21 hours watching T.V.*

If you wish to make a difference to the world, and to leave a positive legacy when you die, then focus on the welfare of your own family.

It is all very well to complain about problems present elsewhere in the world today, but what often matters is the effort you make to address those same problems with your family members.

For instance, if you are concerned about the limited time that parents devote to their children today, then start by changing the allocation of time in your own family. If drug-taking amongst teenagers today concerns you, then ensure that your own children have been given every opportunity to combat the scourge.

We are judged by the actions we take in our own families, not by how we point the finger of blame at others.

The Ripple Effect

Kids don't care what you know until they know you care.

(Jack Canfield)

As a parent, it could be you who sets a child on a path that could change the lives of others. The catalyst may be a simple action, or a seemingly insignificant comment.

On a rainy afternoon, you may casually comment to a twelve-year-old: "That's a fantastic story you've written." A seed is planted, and your daughter eventually pursues media studies. She then progresses to a successful career in magazine editing.

Twenty years later, she is influencing the thinking of thousands of readers. Many of the ripples that you create in the lives of your children can have astounding long-term implications.

Children are our future-in-waiting. If you wish for humanity to continue into the twenty-second century and beyond, then you would dedicate a significant proportion of your efforts to nurturing your children.

Conversely, any civilisation is on a downward spiral to self-destruction once its members consistently abuse their children. The ripples that result from such tragic behaviour will ensure that similar toxic actions will taint the following generation.

The most powerful measurement of a society's soul is the manner in which it treats its children. So, begin with your own family. It is from there that you can spread many long-term ripples for the world's future.

The Ripple Effect

> *People say that what we're all seeking is a meaning of life. I don't think that's what we're really seeking. I think that what we're seeking is an experience of being alive, so that our life experiences on the purely physical plane will have resonances within our innermost being and reality, so that we actually feel the rapture of being alive.*
>
> *(Joseph Campbell)*

You can make a difference to the world if you:

Re-discover your spirit

> When you re-discover your spirit for life, your inner energy will create special ripples every day of your life.

What would you do if you were visited later tonight by an angel, who proceeded to inform you that tomorrow would be the last day of your life? There is only one restriction on the activities. You would not be allowed to break any moral or legal codes.

Is there any chance that you would waste the day away? Not very likely, is it? You would probably cherish every second of your time, making the most of these last opportunities to experience life fully. Imagine all of the ripples that you would set off during that day.

During many of my workshops, I have asked hundreds of people what they would do in this instance. Everyone said they wouldn't waste time consoling themselves over their imminent demise. It would be out of their control.

Many said that they would spend their time with people they love, others claimed that they would engage in their favourite activities, a few said they would reminisce over the good times. But everyone agreed on one thing that they would do.

They would savour each moment of the day, immersing themselves fully in every experience. They would glow with the spirit of being alive, of feeling that there was a substance to everything that they did. On a day such as this, they would re-discover their soul.

Life's a pretty precious and wonderful thing. You can't sit down and let it lap around you...you have to plunge into it, you have to dive through it.

(Kyle Crichton)

So that you nurture your spirit for life through every one of your last days (whether it be one day or ten thousand), perhaps you could consider these suggestions:

- Show up. Choose to be present in your life. Experience the fullness of participation, rather than giving lack-lustre half-efforts. Refuse to accept pale imitations of the real thing.
- Pay attention to what has heart and meaning. Do not be swayed by those who feel threatened by the truth and honesty of your emotions. Feel proud of your passion for the everyday.
- Ask yourself what it is that creates spirit in your life. When is it that you feel the passion to participate in what you are doing? Whatever your answer, make sure that you place it first on your daily list, rather than last.
- Become fully aware, really aware, of something nearby. See it in colour rather than black and white. Open your eyes a little wider than normal, and let in the extra light so you can truly see the details. Open your mouth in an expression of astonishment and awe.
- Enjoy simple pleasures. Sing a song with gusto, dance in a way that releases your body, become enchanted by stories you hear.

Stacey died and went to heaven. When she arrived at the Pearly Gates, she was asked: "Stacey, have you truly been Stacey?" (substitute your own name in this story)

Let the beauty we love

be what we do.

(Rumi)

You can make a difference to the world if you:

Enjoy the work of your life

> Your work is vital for your soul's health, and can create an immediate positive difference for both yourself and others.

Three men were once working on a building site. A visitor approached the first and asked what he was working on. "Can't you see for yourself?" the worker retorted. "I'm struggling away in this horrible heat, cutting out these stone blocks, and hating every moment of it."

When the second worker was asked what he was doing, he responded, "Well, I'm shaping these stone blocks so that they can be used according to the building plans. It's boring work, but at least I'm getting paid well for it."

When the visitor asked the third worker what he was doing, he raised his arms to the sky, and passionately exclaimed: "Look all around you. I'm building a cathedral!"

Work is vital for your soul's health. It can give you a purpose for being alive. When you work, you are spreading ripples among your co-workers, your customers and with total strangers. One of the special satisfactions in life is to know that your work has made a tangible positive difference for both yourself and others.

There is a vital distinction to be made here, and it is the difference between *work* and a *job*. A job is something you do so that you will be paid, and generally it involves a set number of hours of personal effort each day.

Instead of thinking about: How do I earn a living?...how do I survive?... we ought to say, what is it that my experiences teach me that could bring advantage to all humanity?
　　　　　　　(R. Buckminster Fuller)

Work, however, is the contribution you make to the planet before you die. It is what you offer to others with the skills that you have, in order to create a better world. If you are especially lucky, your work and your job are the same thing.

This work may involve either paid employment, or unpaid volunteer help. The latter can involve anything from tending your 90-year-old neighbour's garden, to coaching a junior sports team, to helping in a clean-up campaign.

Volunteer or unpaid work is vital, and spreads invaluable ripples. However, we also need to believe that our paid employment can make a positive difference in the lives of others.

Naturally, we do this work so that we can be paid, but there need to be other significant reasons for gaining satisfaction from these efforts. Why not the pleasure derived from making a difference in the lives of others?

To believe that you are making a positive contribution can re-ignite your passion for whatever work you do, even if it is with a large bureaucracy or organisation. Don't feel overwhelmed just because you are one of thousands. Think instead of the special difference that you could make to someone's life in your daily work.

In every form of employment, there are always opportunities to spread ripples to others. Your chance could arise during your next phone conversation, or while you are making a sale early tomorrow morning. It may be during the next meeting you attend, or while you are supporting a customer during an indecisive moment.

We make a living by what we get,

we live by what we give.

(Winston Churchill)

Just for a moment, look at this issue from the opposite perspective. Do you remember those special occasions when you received exceptional service? Perhaps it was an attendant in a store, or a telephonist when you needed to make an enquiry.

Possibly it was a great teacher who changed your child's life for the better. What about a plumber, or electrician, or carpenter, who obviously loved the work they did for you, and completed the task in your house with a smile on their face? Weren't they the ones that you recommended to your friends?

Now put yourself in their shoes. Wouldn't you want people to feel the same way when they were being served by you? Imagine the pride you would feel in your work, and in yourself, if your customers felt this way about you.

When you discover this sense of accomplishment in your work, you will be living the ripple effect with every person you meet. Your work will be making a positive difference in the lives of countless other people.

If it is delightful to fall in love with one person, just imagine what it is like to fall in love with everyone.

(Eknath Easwaran)

You can make a difference to the world if you:

Spread unconditional love

> All major religions refer to the spiritual experience of unconditional love. In such a state of being, positive ripples will flow naturally from your thoughts and actions.

Let me share with you the most astonishing energy booster. It is also one of the simplest ways to generate ripples from your own thoughts. All you will have to do is sit in a place where people are walking past on a regular basis, such as in a shopping centre, or near a street footpath.

Once you are settled, then begin to project affirming thoughts towards specific people as they move past you. Say the words inside your head at normal speaking speed. To an older woman, you might think: "You have a wonderfully regal bearing." To a small child, it might be: "Your positive attitude to life is fantastic." To a young man, it could be: "Great smile."

Keep looking for the good in those you see, and within a few minutes, you will be surrounded by an aura of inner peace and wellbeing. As you stand up and move away, you will feel as though you are walking on air.

If you can manage to do this activity, you will find yourself tapping into the ultimate life force in the universe. It is unconditional love, the supreme state of being. All religions talk of this energy, whether it be referred to as prana, kundalini or the holy spirit.

The Ripple Effect

Some day, after we have mastered the winds, the waves, the tides and gravity we shall harness the energies of love. Then, for the second time in the history of the world, man will have discovered fire.

(Teilhard de Chardin)

It is the energy that is discovered during the N.D.E. (near-death experience), in which the dying person passes along a tunnel towards an all-consuming light that fills them with the totality of being.

This unconditional love moves far beyond the normal definitions of lust, sex, incidental love and even passionate love. It is the energy that is capable of binding us together, of healing our psychic wounds, of drawing wars to a close.

What is special about this energy is that you do not lose any when you give it away. You gain even more. It is the universal win-win experience.

Yet all that you need to do to create this energy is to project affirming thoughts towards others at every opportunity. Positive ripples will then flow naturally from your thoughts and actions.

The energy of this unconditional love can be demonstrated by the lighting of community candles.

Imagine that you are standing in front of thousands of people at a Christmas carols gathering. Everyone, including you, is holding onto an unlit candle. It is dark, it is outdoors, there is no wind.

You then light your own candle and hold it up. It creates a tiny glow in the large arena. You walk forward, and use your candle to light those of the people in the front row.

They turn around and light those nearby, and so on this goes until thousands of candles have been lit. The entire area eventually is suffused with this beautiful light.

Yet you have not lost any light from your own candle. Rather, you have gained because of your effort in contributing to others.

Some men see things as they are,

and say, why?

I dream of things that never were,

and say, why not?

(George Bernard Shaw)

You can make a difference to the world if you:

Connect @ the Net   (18)

> **Because of the prodigious growth rates of Internet usage, you now have the potential opportunity to influence millions of people while sitting at your computer.**

Would you like to become famous? Then set up a video-cam in your bedroom, and broadcast your daily and nightly activities live on your own web-site. Some of these sites (and there are many) record over fifty thousand hits every day. This, naturally, is one of the quirky elements of the Internet, and raises all sorts of intriguing questions about privacy and voyeurism.

Yet it demonstrates one awesome capacity of our present technology. The Internet now provides individuals with the ability to connect directly with potentially millions of people. Never before has a non-media citizen possessed the tool for legally doing this so easily.

This technology has forever changed the way that we live on this planet. Individuals have been given the personal capacity to register their protest, to control their own investments, to connect directly with the organisation providing the service they require. Power is returning to the people.

This places the concept of the ripple effect in an entirely new light. In ages past, any ripples you created would occur when you met someone in a *physical* sense. This would often only happen with a few people at any one time. Today, you can connect with much greater numbers of people at once.

History points to the fact that it's not the Hitlers of the world who ultimately prevail, it's the little people.
(Archbishop Desmond Tutu)

The Internet has created a form of *electronic* ripple effect. In front of a computer, and armed with sufficient expertise, your personal power is unlimited.

As with most initiatives in life, this application of technology has the potential for good, but also for harm. The harm can be extensive. Contrary to the opinion of some, computers do not have a soul, and never will.

When you meet with someone on a physical level, there are all sorts of brain chemistry functions taking place that offer an emotional context to the interaction. These vital chemical functions do not occur through your computer.

Another negative side of personal netpower is the capacity of a single hacker to create immense disruption anywhere in the world. The incidence of computer viruses is also likely to rise with the increased use of e-mail.

In March 1999, the Melissa virus created significant inconvenience for millions of e-mail users. This in turn spread billions of ripples in the lives of those people and their organisations.

However, on the good side, you have the opportunity to create global connections that would otherwise not have been possible. You could join a chatgroup, and share your opinion with thousands of others. Or write a book, and design a web-site to launch it to the world. Or send e-mail to ruthless tyrants in less developed countries, registering your protest at their actions.

Whatever you can do or dream

you can, begin it.

Boldness has genius, power,

and magic in it.

(Goethe)

And if you're really serious about making your mark, then set up that video in your bedroom. Just make sure that you don't snore in your sleep.

The rate of new discoveries on Earth generally has an exponential doubling effect. For example, the amount of change in the past ten years will now be seen in the next five years. In the 21st century, this means that we will witness 20,000 times the amount of change that was experienced in the 20th century. Eminent futurists and scientists now speak of a near-future that will include:
- *3-dimensional faxes*
- *Portable translation devices*
- *Nano-robots inside our bodies*
- *Humanoid (and very lifelike) servants*
- *Brain implants*
- *Artificial brains*
- *Post-human states of being*

Please feel free to check out the web-site for **The Ripple Effect** *on:*
www.headfirst.com.au/ripples/

We do not remember days,

we remember moments.

(Casare Pavese)

You can make a difference to the world if you:

Live in the present moment

> **Any ripples that you create in your life will begin in the present moment. It is right here and now that you change the world with your actions.**

The only time that you can create change in the world is the moment you are in right now. All ripples begin from this present moment. In fact, the ancient secrets to inner peace and ultimate happiness all rest with this simple statement:

Live in the present moment.

One of my favourite stories offers a suggestion on how to do so. It goes like this:

A businessman once heard of a wise old man who knew the three great secrets to life, and it was said that this wise man lived in a mountain cave in a faraway land.

Because he had grown bored with his lifestyle, the businessman sold his company, and began to search the world for the keeper of these priceless secrets. And finally, high up on a mountain in Tibet, he entered a small cave and met the old man.

"Please, O Wise One," pleaded the former businessman. "I wish to know the three great secrets to life. Are you willing to share them with me?"

Yesterday's history,

tomorrow's a mystery.

But today is a gift, and that's

why we call it the present.

(Anon)

"Certainly," replied the wise one. "Sit down and relax, and I will offer them to you. The first secret is to 'Pay Attention'."

"Really?..." responded his listener, with a quizzical expression on his face. "So what is the second?"

"The second," said the wise man, "is to 'Pay Attention'."

"And the third?"

"Ah, the third is to 'Pay Attention'."

When you fully pay attention to your present action, you will be living in the present moment, the one in which all ripples begin. It is a simple notion to describe, and is an exhilarating state in which to live. Yet it is not always easy to practise this concept in a twenty-first century world that compels you to rush everywhere.

To live in the present moment does not mean that you should not think about what lies up ahead. It is fine to plan for holidays, or a new job, or financial independence. But don't place your daily consciousness there as well. Otherwise, you will never feel as though you have arrived in your life.

Your happiness, your satisfaction, your inner peace, will always seem to be somewhere vaguely up ahead. And as you move towards it, you will merely push these vital things further away from yourself.

Likewise with the past. For while it is important to cherish your special memories from earlier times, you should avoid wanting to live back there. Otherwise, your present reality will never seem to shape up against your past days. You will always feel disappointed, and continue to offer laments such as "It was so much better when..." or "I wish we could go back to...".

> *Millions of persons long for immortality,*
> *who do not know what to do with*
> *themselves on a rainy afternoon.*
>
> *(Anon)*

It is as though you regret that you are alive right now. The interesting thing is that, in the midst of your remorse, you are creating a negative *past* for your future up ahead.

While there are no quick fixes for encouraging yourself to live within the present moment, here are some ideas for steadily developing the capacity to be fully present in the *now*:

- Watch small children at play. They provide a wonderful role model for living in the present moment. Observe the way that they are fully engrossed in their task. It is pure focus. If you would like to experience this feeling, then think of an activity that you loved to do when you were a child…and go out and do it.

- Exercise regularly. The body is always in the present. It is your mind that wanders into the past or the future, creating worry and misgivings. The body stays right here. This is one reason why people love to participate in physical activity, especially after a hard-fought day in the office and the traffic. It helps them to return to their natural state of being present in the moment.

- Observe your pets. Animals live in the *now*. This is one reason why so many of us enjoy having pets in our lives. Animals remind us of how to live in our fully present state. They rarely rush, they do one thing at a time, and they pay full attention to what they are doing, whether it be sleeping, playing or eating.

The Ripple Effect

There are two ways to live your life.

One is as though nothing is a miracle.

The other is as though everything is a miracle.

(Albert Einstein)

- Live *in* the present moment, rather than adopting some teenagers' perspectives on life in which they live *for* the moment. To live *for* the moment is to ignore the past and the future, and perhaps to even treat those times with possible contempt. Rather, live *in* the moment, while still holding respect for past experiences, and taking into account the consequences of your actions in the future.

- Look for the magic in the everyday. See everything for the first time, as though you are a child who is being introduced to the wonders of everyday life. Think back to the experience of being seven years old, and waking up on a Saturday morning in the first day of your holidays. You jumped out of bed, ready to make the most of every moment. Yes, you may now be a sensible adult, but you can still feel this. Trust yourself. Let go. In such a state of being, you will create truly special ripples.

The Ripple Effect

> *I am of the opinion that my life belongs to the community, and as long as I live, it is my privilege to do for it whatever I can. I want to be thoroughly used up when I die, for the harder I work, the more I live. Life is no 'brief candle' for me. It is a sort of splendid torch which I have got hold of for a moment, and I want to make it burn as brightly as possible before handing it on to future generations.*
>
> *(George Bernard Shaw)*

You can make a difference to the world if you:

Bring people together

> When people are brought together in a group, a party, a team, or any community initiative, they have a greater opportunity to create ripples in the lives of others.

One of the most powerful and obvious ways to spread ripples is by physically bringing people together. Ripples rarely operate when you have no contact with other people. They occur when you participate in some form of community experience.

However, in some parts of the world today, it is not as easy as it sounds to join in a community. Surprisingly, in spite of our burgeoning population, we have never been more isolated in human history.

Three hundred years ago, you would have known everyone in your small village, and felt as though you belonged to a common group. Today, many are struggling to recreate this sense of community. The numbers just seem to be too overwhelming.

Particularly in larger cities, a cocoon mentality has been created by a general fear and distrust of the outside world. Homes become fortresses, and are heavily barricaded against the outside world.

As well, modern technological advances have made it easier to create your own cocoon. Paradoxically, these more effective electronic communication systems have led to less effective personal contact.

To slowly turn this around, you could steadily bring small groups of people together whenever possible. Show others how a sense of community can be created in very simple ways.

It takes a whole village

to raise a child.

(African proverb)

And what is a community? It is a group of people that may form for one night, or for many years. A community is formed when everyone is involved and we must keep in mind that the word *everyone* literally means ***every*** single ***one***.

A sense of community can be created at an evening party, or with a sports team established for a full season. It can be seen at a family gathering over a weekend, or with a group that joins together to assist the elderly in your local neighbourhood.

It can even occur during natural disasters or serious accidents, when people will immediately join with others to offer their help to total strangers. If these major emergencies are any indication, we obviously all know intuitively how to link with others and create a supportive community.

If you have ever been involved in such a situation, then you will be aware of the spirit that fills your heart as you carry out your contribution for the group.

It is at such times that you fully discover how enriching it is to make a difference in the lives of others. You will feel that your life is on track, that it has a purpose, and will realise just how powerful the ripple effect can be for your own well-being as well as for others.

Here are some further suggestions for bringing people together in everyday life, and giving them the opportunity to spread ripples amongst others:

The Ripple Effect

> *Example is not the main thing in influencing others — it is the only thing.*
> *(Albert Schweitzer)*

- Establish a Neighbourhood Watch group. All around the world, this community initiative has lowered the incidence of burglary in specific areas. It succeeds because it encourages people who might otherwise be strangers to band together and watch each other's properties.
- Have special Challenge Days with your friends or family, in which each person takes a turn at organising the day's events for everyone else.
- Arrange a clean-up campaign in your area. The ultimate example is Ian Kiernan's Clean Up Australia program, which has now been expanded to Clean Up The World. At the local level, people meet on the first Sunday in March each year, and clear rubbish that is lying around their neighbourhood. Could you arrange a special time in your own area?
- Consult with other community members and submit a funding proposal for a community project to your local council, or to your regional political representative. Although funding grants can sometimes be difficult to acquire, you also may find that politicians are keen to generate support amongst local community groups. It is much cheaper to grant $2000 to a local group, than to pay $20 000 to a professional company to complete the same work. The local people are more likely to contribute free labour, which lowers the expense of the project.
- Organise a party for any reason at all. It could be for a group of friends, or a team of sports fanatics, or family members. Every time that you do this, you are offering people the opportunity to form a mini-community and spread ripples.

When you seek happiness for yourself it will always elude you. When you seek happiness for others you will find it yourself.

(Ancient wisdom)

According to the mathematical principle known as **six degrees of separation,** *there is a maximum of only six people between you and any other person on Earth.*

Thus, if you know forty people, and those forty each know another forty, and so on, you would go no further than six people to connect with anyone else alive today.

Think of how many people you know in your own life, and then consider the people that they would know. Before too long, you will find yourself **connected** *with everyone else in the world.*

The Ripple Effect

> *A pessimist, they say, sees a glass of water as being half-empty; an optimist sees the same glass as half-full. But a giving person sees a glass of water and starts looking for someone who might be thirsty.*
>
> *(G. Donald Gale)*

Some pebbles to toss in the pond:

Things you can do right now

Giving is its own reward.

(Ancient wisdom)

Give a quiet smile (or an overwhelming one, if that is your style) to the next person you pass in the street.

A ripple effect

The recipient, heartened by the warmth of your smile, later apologises to a loved one for negative comments made during a bitter argument earlier that day.

The Ripple Effect

> The social sum total of everybody's little everyday efforts, especially when added together, doubtless releases far more energy into the world than do rare heroic feats.
>
> (Robert Musil)

***Pick up the next ten pieces
of rubbish you see, and
place them into a bin.***

A ripple effect

An overseas visitor, impressed by the cleanliness in the street, eventually arranges for a conference to be held in your city. Over five hundred international delegates attend this conference twelve months later, and inject millions of dollars into your local economy.

*The happiness of life is made up of
the little charities of a kiss or smile,
a kind look, a heartfelt compliment.*
   (Samuel Taylor Coleridge)

Say positive things about someone else in their absence.

A ripple effect

That person later hears about your comments, and is inspired to present her ideas for an innovative program to her employer. Several weeks later, because of her successful presentation, she is promoted to an exciting new position in her company.

> *I long to accomplish a great and noble task, but it is my chief duty to accomplish small tasks as if they were great and noble.*
>
> *(Helen Keller)*

Compliment a shop attendant on his excellent service.

A ripple effect

Boosted by your comments, the attendant gives exemplary service to many other customers throughout the day.

I can't change the direction of the wind.

But I can adjust the sails.

(Anon)

If you see an interesting article, book or news item, send it to someone you know would appreciate it.

A ripple effect

The information allows this person to make a life-changing decision about her next job.

Live your beliefs, and you can turn the world around.

(Thoreau)

***Practise good manners
while driving. Wave courteously
and smile at another driver.***

~~~

A ripple effect

That driver's growing irritation is defused, and a few minutes later, she avoids creating the serious accident that might have occurred had she remained tense and upset.

Meaning is in contribution, in living for something higher than self.

(Stephen Covey)

Write a brief note of support to public authorities who have implemented a worthwhile social welfare program for young people.

~~~~~

A ripple effect

Your encouragement inspires the authorities to persevere with the program, and many young lives are eventually changed for the better.

The ultimate aim of the quest must be the wisdom and the power to help others.

(Joseph Campbell)

***Buy a tiny gift for a good friend,
and send it to them with a note that
simply says "Because you deserve it".***

A ripple effect

Your friend shows the gift to every one
of her visitors that day, who all comment
on the value of friendship in today's society.

*I am only one, but still I am one.
I cannot do everything, but still I
can do something. I will not refuse
to do something I can do.*

(Helen Keller)

Immediately ask someone to stop if you hear them spreading malicious gossip about another person.

A ripple effect

Had the gossip continued to spread, it would have ruined that person's career, and led to the break-up of his relationship with his partner.

In the Middle Ages, the Jewish sage
Moses Maimonides wrote about the
seven levels of charity. All of the levels
are important, but the highest level is to
give unconditionally, anonymously, just
because it is right to give. Give
a gift, big or small, without knowing who
the receiver is and without the recipient
knowing who you are.

(McCarty and McCarty)

Make an immediate donation to a needy charity in your local area.

A ripple effect

Your donation allows them to employ a counsellor for an extra two hours. During this time, the counsellor resolves a potentially serious problem for a young woman who is being supported by the charity.

Sometimes when I consider what tremendous consequences come from little things...I am tempted to think...there are no little things.

(Bruce Barton)

Send a positive written message to anyone who has changed your children's lives in some special way, such as a gifted teacher who has inspired them to exceptional efforts.

A ripple effect

This teacher, who had been pondering alternative career options, is then encouraged to stay in the profession, and continues to motivate thousands of other children in future years.

The Ripple Effect

> *The purpose of life is to matter — to count, to stand for something, to have it make some difference that we lived at all.*
>
> *(Leo Rosten)*

Write small complimentary notes to your family members, and hide them where you know they will find them, such as under their pillow, beside the biscuit container, or inside their school bag.

───⁂───

A ripple effect

They will have a better day, simply because
of the energy that you created in their
heart with your message.

A thought to take away

So there you have it. A range of suggestions on how you can make a difference. Now it's your turn. Think each day of how you can change the world in your own special way, and then simply go out and do it.

Remember! You can make a positive difference with everything you do. In fact, your very next action may be just the one that transforms someone's life. So make every moment count!

References

Bryner, Andy and Markova, Dawna. *An Unused Intelligence: Physical Thinking For 21st Century Leadership.* Berkeley, California: Conari Press, 1996.

Burke, James. *The Pinball Effect.* New York: Little, Brown & Company, 1996.

Combs, Allan and Holland, Mark. *Synchronicity: Science, Myth, and the Trickster.* New York: Paragon House, 1990.

Covey, Stephen. *The 7 Habits Of Highly Effective People.* New York: Simon & Schuster, 1989.

Crum, Thomas. *The Magic Of Conflict: Turning A Life Of Work Into A Work Of Art.* New York: Simon & Schuster, 1987.

Csikszentmihalyi, Mihaly. *Flow: The Psychology Of Happiness.* London: Rider, 1992.

de Mello, Anthony. *The Heart Of The Enlightened.* London: Fount Paperbacks, 1987.

de Mello, Anthony. *Awareness.* London: HarperCollins, 1990.

Diamond, Harvey. *Your Heart Your Planet.* U.S.A.; Hay House Inc., 1990.

Dryden, Gordon and Vos, Jeannette. *The Learning Revolution.* Auckland: Profile Books, 1993.

Dyer, Wayne. *Real Magic: Creating Miracles In Everyday Life.* Sydney: HarperCollins, 1992.

Ellyard, Peter. *Ideas For The New Millennium.* Australia: Melbourne University Press, 1998.

Ferguson, Marilyn. *The Aquarian Conspiracy: Personal and Social Transformation In Our Time.* New York: Tarcher Books, 1980.

Fox, Matthew. *The Re-Invention Of Work.* New York: HarperCollins, 1994.

Frankl, Victor E. *Man's Search For Meaning.* New York: Washington Square Press, 1959.

Fromm, Eric. *The Art Of Loving.* London: Mandala, 1985

Fulgrum, Robert. *All I Really Need To Know I Learned In Kindergarten: Uncommon Thoughts On Common Things.* London: Grafton, 1988.

Hall, Brian. *The Saskiad.* London: Secker & Warburg, 1996.

Handy, Charles. *The Hungry Spirit: Beyond Capitalism. A Quest For Purpose In The Modern World.* London: Random House, 1998.

Hoff, Benjamin. *The Tao Of Pooh.* London: Mandarin, 1982.

Hoff, Benjamin. *The Te Of Piglet.* London: Mandarin, 1992.

Houston, Jean. *A Mythic Life: Learning to Live Our Greater Story.* New York: HarperCollins, 1996.

Larned, Marianne. *Stone Soup For The World.* California: Conari Press, 1997.

Leonard, George. *The Silent Pulse: A Search For The Rhythm That Exists In Each Of Us.* New York: Penguin, 1978.

McLaughlin, Corinne & Davidson, Gordon. *Spiritual Politics: Changing The World From The Inside-Out.* New York: Ballantine Books, 1994.

Moore, Thomas. *Care Of The Soul: A Guide For Cultivating Depth and Sacredness in Everyday Life.* New York: Harper Perennial, 1992.

Osbon, Diane. *Reflections On The Art Of Living: A Joseph Campbell Companion.* New York: HarperCollins, 1991.

Pinkney, Maggie. *More Pocket Positives.* Victoria: Five Mile Press, 1999.

Popov, Linda, Popov, Dan and Kavelin, John. *The Virtues Guide: A Handbook For Parents Teaching Virtues.* Australia: The Virtues Project Inc., 1995.

Redfield, James. *The Celestine Prophecy: An Adventure.* New York: Bantam Books, 1993.

Roddick, Anita. *Body And Soul.* London: Vermilion, 1992.

Ryan, Tony. *Wrapped In Living: 20 Gifts For Creating Passion In Your Life.* Brisbane: HeadFirst Publishing, 1996.

Senge, Peter. *The Fifth Discipline: The Art And Practice of the Learning Organization.* Sydney: Random House, 1990.

Waitley, Dennis and Matheson, Boyd. *Attitude: Your Internal Compass.* U.S.A.: Successories Library.

Wallis, Jim. *The Soul Of Politics: A Practical and Prophetic Vision for Change.* New York: Fount Paperbacks, 1994.

APPENDIX I

Origin of the ripples concept

No single person can say that they first thought of the ripple effect. It is everyone's idea. We all know, with the wisdom developed throughout human history, that our everyday actions ripple out and affect other people.

The ripples idea has formed in my own thinking from a variety of sources:

- As I grew up, my parents always told me how I could make a difference to the world with what I did.
- In history lessons during my teenage years, I became intrigued by the domino principle, which explained how difficulties in one country could lead to the fall of political and economic systems in other countries.
- Over twenty years ago, as I studied to become a teacher, several lecturers told me that to be a teacher was to make a difference to the lives of children.
- When I entered teaching, I constantly thought about the everyday ways that I could help children to discover their lifelong potential. I believe that it was the little things I did that often made a significant difference.
- Throughout my life, I have encountered the expression the *ripple effect* in news reports, in magazine articles, in everyday conversations with countless other people. The *ripple effect* is all around me, and you, and every person on this planet.

APPENDIX II
About the author

Tony Ryan is an Australian writer, public speaker and workshop presenter who travels extensively throughout the world with his work. He is a former teacher who passionately believes in the capacity of each person to make a tangible difference to the quality of life on this planet.

Tony is the author of fourteen books and activity manuals on effective thinking and learning. These titles include:

- *Mindlinks*
- *Brainstorms*
- *Thinkfest*
- *Thinkers Keys For Kids*
- *The Clever Country Kits*
- *Special Occasions*
- *Wrapped In Living*

Conference Seminar Presentations

Tony Ryan is available to present keynote addresses at conferences, and to facilitate seminars on many of the issues raised in this book. These issues can include:

- innovative thinking
- lifelong learning
- teamwork dynamics
- workplace enthusiasm.

If you would like Tony to encourage people to believe that they can make a difference with the work that they do, then please feel free to contact HeadFirst Publishing. Our details:

Phone: 61 07 3411 5451
Fax: 61 07 3411 5621
Email: tonyryan@headfirst.com.au